A Colony of
Ants
and Other Insect Groups

Anna Claybourne

Raintree

www.raintreepublishers.co.uk

Visit our website to find out more information about Raintree books.

To order:

☎ Phone 0845 6044371

📄 Fax +44 (0) 1865 312263

💻 Email myorders@raintreepublishers.co.uk

Customers from outside the UK please telephone +44 1865 312262

Raintree is an imprint of Capstone Global Library Limited, a company incorporated in England and Wales having its registered office at 7 Pilgrim Street, London, EC4V 6LB – Registered company number: 6695582

Edited by Nancy Dickmann, Adam Miller, and Laura Knowles
Designed by Richard Parker
Picture research by Ruth Blair
Original Illustrations © Capstone Global Library Ltd 2013
Illustrations by Jeff Edwards
Originated by Capstone Global Library Ltd
Printed and bound in China by CTPS

ISBN 978 1 406 23946 1 (hardback)
16 15 14 13 12
10 9 8 7 6 5 4 3 2 1

British Library Cataloguing in Publication Data
Claybourne, Anna.
A colony of ants and other insect groups.
-- (Animals in groups)
  595.7'156-dc22
A full catalogue record for this book is available from the British Library.

Acknowledgements
We would like to thank the following for permission to reproduce photographs: Alamy pp. 22 (© blickwinkel, 33 (© neil setchfield yuckfood.com); Corbis pp. 13 (© Alex Wild/Visuals Unlimited), 27 (© Michael & Patricia Fogden); Dreamstime.com p. 26 (© Gordon Miller); iStockphoto pp. 15 (© Henrik Larsson), 25 (© Focus_on_Nature); Naturepl pp. 9 (© Nature Production), 21 (© Mark Bowler), 23 (© Bence Mate), 30 (© Visuals Unlimited), 31 (© Meul / ARCO); Science Photo Library pp. 17 (NATURE'S IMAGES), 19 (MONA LISA PRODUCTION/), 39 (SALLY BENSUSEN), 41 (PASCAL GOETGHELUCK); Shutterstock pp. 4 (© Andrey Pavlov), 5, 8, 18 (© Christopher Tan Teck Hean), 7 (© xfox01), 11 (© AlexGul), 12 (© Falk Kienas), 16 (© Juha Sompinmäki), 28, 32 (© Henrik Larsson), 35 (© vblinov), 36 (© Daniel Prudek), 37 (© Ratikova).

Cover photograph of leafcutter ants reproduced with permission of Alamy (© Picture Press).

Every effort has been made to contact copyright holders of any material reproduced in this book. Any omissions will be rectified in subsequent printings if notice is given to the publisher.

Contents

DID YOU KNOW?

Discover amazing facts about ants.

HUMAN INTERACTION

Find out what happens when humans and ants come into contact with each other.

Some words are shown in bold, **like this**. You can find out what they mean by looking in the glossary.

HABITAT IN DANGER

Learn how some ants' habitats are under threat, and what is being done to protect them.

Welcome to the colony!

Ants are amazing animals. They're tiny – less than a millionth of the size of a human being. But they're extremely strong, with superhuman senses and great communication skills. They can share tasks, work together in a team, and pass on complicated messages. Scientists still aren't sure how they manage some of their incredible feats!

What is an ant?

An ant is a type of insect. Like all insects, ants have three main body parts, six legs, and a pair of **antennae**, or feelers. Scientists have discovered around 12,500 ant **species**, ranging in size from about 1 millimetre (0.04 inches) to 5 centimetres (2 inches) long.

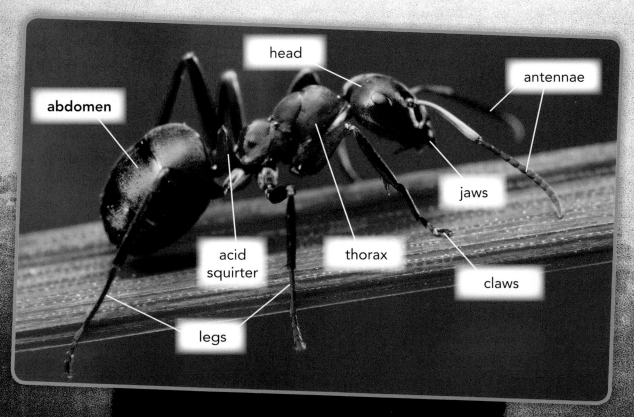

In this close-up photo of a wood ant, you can clearly see its main body parts.

HUMAN INTERACTION

Ants can be a nuisance for humans. They often steal our food and invade our homes. For every human being on Earth, scientists think there are up to a million ants.

Ants are "social insects". They live together in big groups, called **colonies**, and share the jobs they need to do to survive. They take turns at tasks such as finding food, digging tunnels, or guarding the nest. One ant, the queen, lays eggs for the colony, and the others look after the babies. A colony can have the same population of ants as humans in a big city!

These ants are working together to carry a piece of food back to their nest.

DID YOU KNOW?

Driver ants (also called safari ants) have enormous colonies. One colony can contain more than 20 million ants!

Why do ants live together?

Living in a group makes sense for ants. Sharing a nest and food protects them from danger and starvation, much better than if they lived alone.

Ants will fight to defend other members of their colony. An individual ant may even die fighting to protect the others. That's not very good news for that ant, of course! But it does mean that each ant has thousands of others looking out for it. Baby ants and the queen are especially well protected. This makes sure that the colony can keep going, even if it is attacked.

Not just ants

It's not only ants that live in big groups – some other insects such as bees, wasps, and termites do, too. So do humans, in a way. You don't have to grow all your own food or write your own schoolbooks! Instead, each person has their own job to do, and people do things for each other.

DID YOU KNOW?

Some scientists think that an ant colony works almost like one "super-**organism**". It's like a giant creature, made up of many tiny, separate parts. Some even compare an ant colony to a human brain. Ants don't think about their decisions in the same way that people do, but a whole ant colony together can have a similar number of brain cells to one human brain.

To us, ants may look as if they are running around randomly, but they are all busy doing jobs, communicating and helping each other.

7

Different shapes

In each ant species, there are several different types of ant, known as **castes**. Each caste has its own role to play in the colony. The castes are often different sizes, and may also look different.

Who's who?

Ant castes include queens, males, and worker ants. In a typical colony, there are lots of workers, but just one queen and a few males.

The queen is an egg machine. Although she's called the queen, she doesn't really rule the colony. She just lays eggs, which the workers carry away and care for.

These forest ants are both the same species, and both worker ants. But the bigger one is a soldier, while the other is a normal worker.

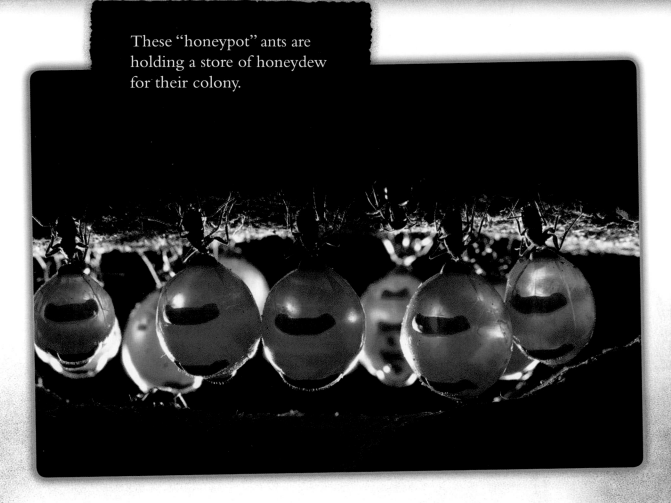

These "honeypot" ants are holding a store of honeydew for their colony.

A male ant's job is to leave the nest and **mate** with a new queen, so that new colonies can start. Only a few male ants are born in a colony each year. As they have to search far and wide for a mate, they have wings.

Worker ants are the "normal" ants you see scurrying around. They are all female. There can be several different sizes of worker ant in a colony, and some may also have special features. Soldier ants are workers with extra-large jaws, for fighting enemies. In some species, a few workers are used as storage jars! Other workers feed them a food called **honeydew** (see page 26) and they swell up to the size of grapes. They hang from a tunnel roof deep in the nest, until the food is needed. They can pass it back out through their mouths to the other ants.

Ants are everywhere

Wherever you live in the world, you're probably no stranger to ants. They are found almost everywhere on our planet, except in the deep oceans and the freezing polar regions.

Scientists think ants have existed for around 150 million years. Over time, they have spread out across most of the world, and developed into thousands of different species. Ants are super-survivors, and have adapted, or changed, to suit all kinds of different **habitats**.

HABITAT IN DANGER

A few ant species are **endangered** because of damage to their habitats. The Sri Lankan relict ant is one. It is at risk because its forest habitat in Sri Lanka has been cleared and broken up.

The Sahara Desert ant lives in burrows in the desert sand, and can come out to search for food even in temperatures above 50 degrees Celsius (122 degrees Fahrenheit). That is hotter than a very hot bath! This ant is one of the most heat-resistant animals on Earth. Its body makes **chemicals** that prevent it from becoming too hot.

One type of ant, the beachcomber ant, is adapted to survive underwater. It digs underground nests in the seaside mud, and when the tide comes in, the nests get flooded. The ants survive by trapping pockets of air in their nest chambers. They can also swim and "skate" on the water surface.

These desert ants are braving
the heat of the Sun to leave
their nest and search for food.

A place to live

As they work together to build their nests, ants create some of the most amazing animal homes in the world. They can have thousands of connected tunnels and neatly arranged chambers.

A typical ant home is an underground nest in the soil or sand. The ants dig out the underground tunnels and rooms, and carry all the dirt they remove up to the surface. This makes an anthill – a heap of sand or soil that forms the upper part of the nest.

If you see a large, smooth, round mound like this in a garden or forest, it is almost certainly an anthill.

DID YOU KNOW?

In Brazil in 2004, scientists filled an empty leafcutter ants' nest with concrete, then cleared away the soil around it. They found it reached 8 metres (26 feet) underground and contained more than 7,000 chambers.

Unusual nests

Some species have other ways of making a home. Here are a few of them:

- Weaver ants glue living leaves together in trees, using silk from an ant **larva** (baby).
- Some army ants are **nomadic**, which means they move from place to place, and have no fixed home. Sometimes, they all clump together and form a cosy nest made from their own bodies!
- Some ant colonies live inside "ant plants", such as myrmecodias. These plants have a swollen base full of hollow tunnels where ants can live. In return, the ants' droppings provide the plant with **nutrients** that help them grow.

These Argentine ants are scurrying along the tunnels in their nest.

How do ants communicate?

Ants living together in a colony have to be able to communicate. The main way they do this is by using special chemicals (substances) that they release from their bodies.

An ant's body can release many different message chemicals, known as **pheromones**. Each one has its own scent, or smell. Other ants pick up the scent using their antennae.

How do they do it?

Ants have special body parts, called glands, that make pheromones. Some are in the head or antennae, some in the abdomen, and some, such as the poison gland, are in the tail. The glands make the pheromones and release them on to the ant's body surface. The pheromones can escape into the air, or rub off on to the ground to leave a chemical trail.

An ant uses its ultra-sensitive antennae to spot different pheromones. They send the sense signals to the ant's brain, so that it gets the message. Ants wave their antennae in the air, use them to track a trail along the ground, or touch other ants to pick up signals. They can also taste food with them. The antennae sense is a bit like our senses of taste and smell combined.

DID YOU KNOW?

Ants cannot see very well. Most species have poor eyesight, and in some species, the workers are completely blind.

Unlike most other insects, an ant's antennae are "elbowed", meaning they have joints in the middle. This helps ants position their antennae and move them around more easily.

What do ants say?

Ants send many different kinds of chemical messages. Here are some of them:

- *This way to the food!:* Ants show the way to a good source of food using a chemical trail along the ground.

- *I'm your friend:* Ants can tell which other ants belong to their own colony by their pheromones.

- *The queen is safe:* The queen constantly makes pheromones to let all the other ants know that she's alive and laying eggs.

- *This is my job:* Each ant releases chemicals to tell others its role, such as baby-feeder or nest-builder.

You can often see ants following a pheromone trail to and fro between a food source.

A bullet ant checks out a beetle to see whether it poses a threat to the ant colony.

- *No food here:* If a food source has run out, or a pathway leads to a dead end, a pheromone can tell other ants not to bother going that way.

- *Danger alert!:* An alarm pheromone warns other ants of a threat, and asks for help.

- *Hey, get off me!:* If an ant is attacked by enemy ants, it will release strong-smelling pheromones to warn them off.

DID YOU KNOW?

Some ants use pheromones to trick other ants. When invading another colony, they can copy their enemies' pheromone and pretend to belong to the nest to avoid attack. Or they release "propaganda pheromones" that confuse their enemies, making them attack each other instead of the invaders.

Ant eyes

While some ants are blind, many do have eyes. A typical ant has two large **compound eyes**, made of lots of small sections. It also has three much smaller eyes on the top of its head, called **ocelli**. The compound eyes are better at seeing, and ants can use them to spot landmarks and food. The ocelli can detect light and dark, and the position of the Sun, but cannot see clearly.

Getting in touch

Ants use their antennae to detect chemical messages, but they also use them to touch and stroke each other. This helps to spread chemical signals around the colony. Scientists think it may be used to pass on other messages, too.

Two ants meet on a rose to rub their antennae together and "kiss", or exchange food and chemical messages with their mouths.

A scientist watches as ants choose pathways through a set of mazes to learn more about how they communicate.

Feel the vibrations

Ants can also use sounds to communicate, though they do not "speak" using their mouths. Instead they rub sections of their abdomens together to make sounds called stridulations. The other ants can "hear" the sounds by sensing the vibrations through the ground. Stridulations can be used as an alarm call, a distress call when one ant needs help, or to call workers together.

DID YOU KNOW?

In experiments, scientists have found that an ant can work out how to get through a maze. It can then pass this information on to another ant. Some species of ants seem to do this by touching their antennae together.

Scout on the lookout

The ants in a colony work together to collect food. They don't all run everywhere at once, looking for food wherever they can find it. Instead, to save time and energy, "scout" ants go out first. They mainly use their antennae to sniff out food sources.

When a scout has found some food, it lays a pheromone trail, showing the other ants where to go. Soon, hundreds or thousands of ants start trekking to the food and taking it back to the nest, bit by bit. As they go, they all leave pheromones too, making the trail stronger.

Two wood ant workers feed a larger queen ant (the one with wings), by passing her food from their own mouths.

Taste this!

Ants often put their mouths together to pass food to each other. This is sometimes called "kissing", though it isn't really kissing. Ants do it to share food with other colony members, and to show other ants what kind of food they have found. It's also a good way to pass on message pheromones, which are mixed in with the food.

Leafcutter ants use their jaws to cut sections of leaves from plants, then carry the pieces up in the air as they march home along their trail.

DID YOU KNOW?

Leafcutter ants follow long trails up trees or into fields to cut off pieces of leaf, which they carry home to their nests. They don't eat the leaves, but chop them into smaller and smaller pieces, and use them to grow a special fungus that they use as food.

A queen is born

To make new queens, the workers give some larvae extra food. These larvae grow wings, and become fertile, meaning they can have babies. The new queens leave the nest, and fly around looking for a male ant to mate with. This is called the nuptial flight. Once a queen and a male ant have mated, the male dies, and the queen can start a new colony.

Ant colonies release lots of winged male and female ants at the same time. This means that ants from different colonies can meet and mate.

The queen finds a safe place, sheds her wings, and starts laying eggs. She has to care for the first set of eggs and larvae herself. Once they become adults, they look after her. From now on, the queen sits in her chamber in the nest, sleeps, eats food brought to her by the workers, and lays eggs so that the colony can grow.

How many queens?

Although most ant colonies have one queen, not all do. Some can have many queens at the same time, and a few species have no queen at all. Instead, their female workers can lay eggs when they are needed.

Ant queens usually look like normal ants, but bigger. This is a yellow meadow ant queen, surrounded by much smaller workers.

Did you know?

Some ant queens can live for up to 10 years. Army ant queens lay the most eggs – up to 4 million of them every month!

Do other insects live in groups?

Scientists have discovered over a million species of insects. Most of them do not live in large groups, but those that do include most ants, most termites, and some types of bees and wasps.

Wasps

Wasps are closely related to ants. Like ants, they have a sting, a narrow "wasp waist", and biting jaws. The common wasp, or yellowjacket – the type that buzzes around your picnic – lives in a colony, and communicates using chemicals, as ants do. A wasp colony has a queen (sometimes more than one), males, and female workers. The biggest wasp colonies have up to 20,000 wasps in them.

Adult wasps feed on sweet food such as sugar or plant nectar. They also hunt other insects, and collect any other food they can find, to take back to their nest and feed to their larvae.

Common wasps make their nest in a tree, a hole in the ground, or sometimes an old shed or the roof space of a house. They scrape bits of wood from trees, fences, or garden furniture, chew it up, and mix it with their saliva (spit). This makes a papery substance a bit like papier mâché, which they use to build a round nest filled with chambers, or **cells**.

HUMAN INTERACTION

Humans learnt how to make paper from wood by watching wasps chewing wood to make their papery nests.

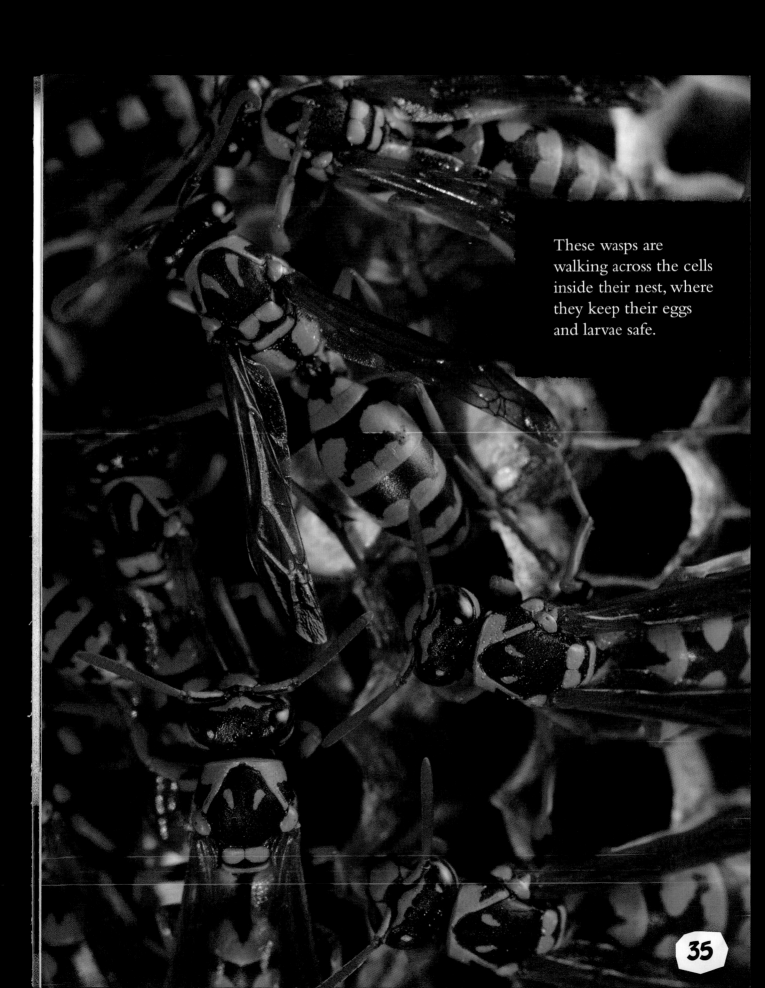

These wasps are walking across the cells inside their nest, where they keep their eggs and larvae safe.